Journey of the Prodigal Daughter

AGNES SCHULTZ

Purelilly Press

First Printing, 2023

JOURNEY OF THE
PRODIGAL DAUGHTER

Contents

Dedication

This book is dedicated to my Aglow chapter, Nasa Aglow, and all my Aglow sisters.

Forward

Agnes Schultz's beautiful book, Journey of the Prodigal Daughter, will be an inspiration to you. You feel the pain she endured during her childhood and early years of her life. You will even cry with her as she candidly pours out her heart to share how she was searching for love and acceptance in all the wrong places. You will rejoice with her as she shares how she found total fulfillment in the love of the Lord and all He had for her future life. She shares how through it all the Lord had never given up on her, even though she had made some wrong choices in life. She learned He still had His hand on her, placing the right people in her life path, leading her back to Him and bringing her into His grace of salvation. As He turned her life around, He gave her "beauty for ashes." She encourages each one of us to walk with the Lord each day through His Word allowing Him to love us, change us, mold us and make us into His image in the way we should live.

I believe there is an anointing on this book and

written under the inspiration of Holy Spirit. I believe everyone who reads this book, especially those suffering from a broken-heart, disappointments and feeling alone, will be healed and restored by the Holy Spirit. You will come to know the great love the Lord has for you as He touches your heart, setting you free. This should be considered a gift to be given to your children, your grandchildren, all your family and friends. This will encourage them to come, give their lives to Jesus and walk with Him all the days of their lives, for He will carry them through it all. We give Him all the praise, glory and honor for the glory of our Abba Father God, in Jesus' Name.

Lorene Kelling, President
NASA Aglow Lighthouse
Webster, Texas

Chapter 1

Do You Hear Me God?

As I sat on the old, dead log, I was thinking to myself and I prayed, "God, why? How did I get here? I feel so lost and broken. I know I have run from You and my calling and ignored the purpose You have for my life, but do I deserve this?" I remembered that in the Bible there was a scripture that said that a believer cannot leave an unbelieving spouse, 'for by them they will be saved.' Could this be right? "Lord, you have seen the beatings I have taken, the continual constant abuse. Is this right? Is this my lot in life? Is this punishment for my sins? Oh God, please help! I do not think I can take it anymore." ...

What did I do or say to set him off this time?! I remember saying that I wanted to go to church, but where did all that rage come from? And what does he mean about me and the preacher having an affair? I don't even know the man, why would I have an affair with him? I just started going there a couple of weeks ago, and the boys are always with me. I don't even know the pastor's name yet! Then, out of nowhere, WHAM, he knocks me to the floor.

"Oh, please God, make the beatings stop! How can he say he loves me in one breath and beat me in the next one? I don't understand. I try to do everything he asks of me. I don't talk back or raise my voice. I keep a clean house and take care of our sons. Oh God, please, I can't take it anymore. I wish I could die."

Chapter 2

Collateral Damage

My boys, Smokey, and Zach had run off to the safety of their room until the shouting and hitting stopped, and finally I was able to escape out to the woods behind the house for just a few minutes. There were usually only a few moments to pull myself together. I was so lost and beaten down; I felt like I had died inside. I didn't even know who I was anymore. I used to be so brave and outspoken, but that part of me was gone. Sometimes I wished he would just kill me and get it over with, and then I would think of my two precious boys and my survival instinct would kick in. *I have to make it, for them*, I thought. I couldn't leave; I felt stuck. He had told me time and time again that I could not leave him and take his boys away, that they needed their father. Being a woman who believed in God and family and making it work, I rationalized staying with him and believed that boys need a father.

Ronnie used to tell me I was beautiful and smart, but all of that had changed. He used to make me feel wanted and loved, then it slowly and subtly changed. "You can't do anything right; you are so stupid," he said. With the beatings, there were also threats. He told me that he would go through everyone he had to, to get to me if I ever left him. He said he would kill my parents, my brothers, anyone that stood in his way, and the sad thing is, I honestly believed he would. I had seen him threaten his own mother at her house.

We were at his mother's house for a visit, and he got mad at me for something. Who knows what it was? The next thing I knew his mom was shoving her way between us as he was going to hit me. He raised his hand to hit her, and I pushed her out of the way, begging her to not get in the middle of it. I knew it was her or me, and she was old. That day he beat me badly, and I ran out of the house, trying to run away but did not have time to grab my first-born son, who was only a few months old at the time. I didn't go far. I was hiding behind a neighbor's house when I heard him screaming at me, "I'm going to stab him if you don't come back, now!" As I peeked around the corner, to my horror, I saw him holding our son by the neck with a large butcher knife to the top of his head, threatening to stab him in the skull with it. My poor precious son, my innocent child. I knew he would do it, and I had to return to stop him! I ran back to the house and begged him to forgive me and to give me my son. He gave him to me. I grabbed my son and held him close, and the rest of the day was a blur. All I cared about was my son was safe, and his mom and I were safe, and at that moment, nothing else mattered.

Rage was a natural thing for Ronnie; anything or nothing could set him off. If I said something, I would get beaten. If I said nothing, he beat me. I was beaten for simple things like if I put leftovers in the refrigerator. I also got beaten if I threw them out and wasted them! I was beaten and I was accused of sleeping with everyone from his brother to our next-door neighbor and even the mail carrier. I never did cheat. I never gave anyone a second glance. I made sure not to give anyone a second glance, and not just for fear of accusation, which always led to a beating. I had deep Christian beliefs that I was guided by, and it simply wasn't in my makeup. I was taught from a child to be faithful to my spouse, and I was.

Chapter 3

The Honeymoon Cycle

I tried to leave Ronnie a few times, but he would always convince me to come back with his promises to never do it again. He would tell me how much he loved me, convincing me that no one could ever love me as much as he did. He told me so a million times. And he usually said he was sorry afterwards, after his explosive attacks. It was never his fault, though. He was sure to tell me what I did to bring on his rage, and how I made him do it. He told me that a million times, fully convincing me that I was the problem.

In the beginning, I know I truly believed that Ronnie loved me, in his own way. I remember when we first met. Although I had been raised believing in God, something in my personal identity about God loving me was lacking. I was looking for love and acceptance in the wrong places, from the wrong people. I was lost in false acceptance and lovely lies.

On the night I met Ronnie, I remember that I was hanging out with one of his friends, John, and with my ex-boyfriend, Joe. At that time, I was making and selling drugs. I had been raised Christian, but I did not know who I was in Christ. I was truly lost and drugged up. My whole world revolved around whoever I was with, but I was never satisfied nor fulfilled.

So, when Ronnie told me he loved me the first time he saw me, that was all I needed. I was looking for love, and that was all I had to hear. I was looking for love in all the wrong places. I had recently found out that Joe had cheated on me, and we had been living together for three years. I was devastated. My world fell apart, and I didn't care about anything or anyone; I went rogue. I left Joe and moved back to my parents' house, searching for something. I dated a couple of different guys, even got engaged to one of them, but it didn't last. I searched for God and made the decision to become a Christian and get saved during this time period. Nothing changed overnight; I still had a rebellious streak in me and not committing my daily walk to God meant that things went from bad to worse. (More on that later.)

So, back to the story, along comes Ronnie at exactly

the wrong time saying what I wanted to hear. He spoke so tenderly. He told me I was beautiful and that he had loved me from the first time he saw me, and he loved me now. He told me I was the only woman he could ever love, and that no one would ever love me as much as he did. He convinced me that night to stay with him and be his woman. He promised to love me and take care of me for the rest of my life, and that's exactly what I wanted and needed to hear.

We continued in our "gangsta" lifestyle with the needles, drugs, and guns until I became pregnant with my first son. I stopped taking the drugs for a short time until he was born. After my son was born, I started back, and I did 'speed' a few times, and then I became pregnant with my second son three months later. By then I was in a prison of my own making. My own insecurities had brought me there.

Sitting back on that log, I cried out to God and prayed, "God help me! I need you! I am so lost without You!" I don't know how long I sat there on that log behind our trailer, but I knew I could not stay there any longer. I only had moments to pull myself together. I knew that my kids needed me, and my husband would not have let me stay away for long, as I was not only a wife, but the cook and the maid. No matter what I did, good or bad, I got beat.

I thought to myself, *that is what I'm good for -*

beatings. My title as Ronnie's wife meant instead of being loved and cherished, I was someone for him to take out his frustrations. The definition of wife for Ronnie seemed to mean that I was his whipping post and using me that way seemed to be the only outlet for all his anger. In my mind, there was no way out.

Chapter 4

The Escape Clause

Ronnie and I were married at the courthouse when I was eight months pregnant with our first son. I was a new Christian and did not know the word of God very well. I only knew a few scriptures, which only represented a partial truth to what God had to say about my marriage. For the little bit I knew, I believed that I was bound to my husband Ronnie, and, according to my faith and what I believed was in the Bible, as a believer I could not leave him (an unbeliever) even if he beat me. This was not true, and I know now that I did not know the Bible very well and had no idea there was an escape clause. I did not know that God had no intention of requiring me or my children to stay in such an unhealthy situation. According to the Bible in the book of Malachi, the Bible says the following:

Malachi 2:13-16 (Amplified 1965)

."...and this you do with double guilt, you cover the altar of the Lord with tears [shed by your unoffending wives, divorced by you that you may take heathen wives], and with your own weeping and crying out because the Lord does not regard your offering anymore or accept it with favor at your hand. Yet you ask, why does He reject it? Because the Lord has witness [to the covenant made at your marriage] between you and the wife of your youth, against whom you have dealt treacherously and to whom you were faithless. Yet she is your companion and the wife of your covenant [made by your marriage vows]. And did not God make [you and your wife] one [flesh]? Did not One make you and preserve your spirit alive? And why did God make you two one? Because He sought a godly offspring [from your union]. Therefore, make heed to yourselves, and let no one deal treacherously and be faithless to the wife of his youth. For the Lord, the God of Israel, says: I hate divorce and marital separation, and him who covers his garment [his wife] with violence. Therefore, keep a watch upon your spirit [that it may be controlled by My Spirit], that you deal not treacherously and faithlessly [with your marriage mate].'

Nobody wants to talk about abuse, even in the church. Maybe they are afraid of offending someone, or maybe they just don't want to get involved. But God does not want anyone to be abused, physically, sexually, or emotionally. God is love and loves you, and I believe abuse of any kind breaks His heart.

God heard my prayer that day, or was it the prayers of my mom, who had always been interceding for me? I don't know if it was one or both, but I know God heard.

Chapter 5

Wakeup Call

He yelled, "You woke me up with your noise!" It was 10 a.m. We were shocked and scared as he grabbed his belt and went after our oldest son, who was only four years old. He beat him with his belt for waking him up as I cried and begged him to stop. Then he grabbed my youngest, who had just turned three, and did the same to him. When he finished with them, he put them in their room and started beating on me.

That was the day I changed. I had taken the beatings for five long years, but now he was starting on my babies, and I had to do something! Something in me woke up. I don't know if it was God giving me the strength or motherly instinct for my boys kicking in, or maybe a little of both, but I knew I had to change our circumstances.

The next day, when I bathed them and saw the bruises, from their waist to their feet, it confirmed what I knew in my gut: something had to change; we had to leave. I knew I had to leave. I could not stay. If not for my sake, and if I could not do it for myself, I at least had to do it for theirs.

I had left before, and he would beg and plead and convince me that it would never happen again, and I would go home. When he wasn't in a rage, things were good, or so I told myself. We lived in the country. We raised pigs and chickens and rabbits and even had a nice garden growing. My boys had a mother and father who loved them, and they were able to play outside and be boys. This is the picture I had of us, and I wanted it to be that way all the time, but this truth was losing its power against the truth of what was actually happening to my boys.

Someone called the cops once when we were visiting his parents. The neighbors heard all the commotion, and when the sheriff's department showed up, they talked to each of us but did nothing else to help. I believe back then (in the 80's) no one understood domestic violence, and I knew that if I pressed charges, sooner or later, he would get out, and he would kill me. I felt helpless. I believed that even the police thought we, the abused women, stayed because we liked it. What they didn't know was that I felt trapped, first emotionally and then physically. Ronnie had made it so that I was not allowed to go anywhere without his permission. Although, I really didn't have anywhere to go. He had slowly alienated me from all my friends and family, and this had been going on for years. Even going to my parents' house was barely allowed. The only reason I was able to see my parents was because we stored clothes in their attic. Any place I would go was timed by him. For example, if I had to go to the store, or to my parents' house, it was only for a small, limited time for a specific reason. If I were not back when he said to be back, I would have gotten beaten for it.

Everything in me changed. I was so scared when I saw what he had done to our babies. I knew I had to do something. Now that he had done it once, I knew he would do it again, and I could not let that happen; I had to plan an escape.

Chapter 6

The Plan

The next time I was able to visit my parents came a few days later. It was the beginning of June. The weather was warming up, so it was time to put away our winter clothes and get out the summer ones. Every year, at the beginning of the shift of each season, I would pack up the children's clothes from the previous season and go get the clothes I had previously packed up out of my mom's attic. My boys had a lot of clothes, thanks mostly to hand-me-downs from Ronnie's sister and my mom's friends. I asked him if I could switch out the clothes, and he allowed me to go for two hours, which didn't give me much time. It took me 45 minutes to get there, so I only had about 30 minutes to get the clothes and talk to my parents. I went early the next morning because my dad worked the graveyard shift; that way, I could talk to both parents together. It was hard for me, but I had to tell them all about all the beatings, and when I showed them the bruises on the boys, they were totally ready to help. They had no idea I had been going through these beatings all along, although they knew something wasn't right. Together, we devised a plan: I would wait till Ronnie was in a good mood and approach him about going to make the big switch of clothes. I hoped he would not suspect me of planning an escape. The plan involved moving to Colorado where my oldest brother lived. I would have to take a bus, which would take a couple of days. My mother agreed to take care of all the details. The big problem was the timing. We didn't know when I would be able to get back to Mommas, but we had a plan, and we would work on it. We knew that we would have to act fast because it would all be on the spur of the moment.

So, in the meantime, I went home with the boys and began to systematically clear some things out. I wanted to remove any connections between me and where I was going. I had to get rid of all the phone bills that might have my sister or brother's phone numbers and get rid of cards and letters from my sister, Sheila, who had sent me packages and letters over the years. All the while being careful not to let him know what I was up to. I was even able to get some of my extra clothes to my parents' house so we would have clothes to bring with us. I knew that was all we could bring with us. Anything else missing from our house, like household items, would set off alarms in his mind. We had one vehicle at the time, my old blue 1966 Ford step side pickup, which I would have to leave behind at my parents' house. How I loved that truck, but sacrifices had to be made, and it would not make it all the way to Colorado anyway.

Meanwhile, Ronnie and I had discussed getting a second car. We had discussed needing another vehicle, and a friend was going to give us a car that needed some repairs. My husband Ronnie had decided that he was going to work on it and get it running for me. The car was at their house, a couple of streets away, and he had planned to spend the entire day working on it. I saw this as the opportunity I had been waiting for!

I drove Ronnie to my friend's house to work on the car. The boys and I would spend the day visiting with my parents. I drove him to the house where he would be working on the car the entire day. When I dropped him off, I raced back to my house to grab a couple more boxes of clothes and my dog, Tina; a small little Peekapoo dog that barely weighed five pounds. I knew I couldn't leave her; he had kicked her across the room one day at his mother's house and nearly killed her. I remember he knocked her out, thinking he had killed her. I held her in my arms and prayed and cried. Thank God, she revived. There was no way that I could leave her with him.

I was terrified the whole time that he would catch

me. My mind raced as I reviewed my actions. I hoped that I was careful enough not to raise suspicions. Had Ronnie caught me going back to get my little dog Tina, he would have surely guessed that something was up. When I got to Mom's, she was home alone. My dad was working the day shift this week and wouldn't be home until 3:45 pm. So, she and I got the boxes of clothes organized to take, and as we discussed the plan, I got increasingly nervous.

My Mom's cousin was the local Chief of Police at that time, and she called him and asked him to come over. This caught the attention of the State Trooper that lived down the street from my parents' house, and he came over as well. Interestingly enough, a Sheriff's Deputy that was passing by also stopped in. It was surreal; I knew now that God was protecting my family.

I told the police the whole story and told how he threatened to go into my parents' house and kill everyone to get to me. I was leaving the truck in their backyard so he would assume I was there. I didn't want to leave it but had no other option. We told the officers that we were going to wait for my dad to get off work to drive us to the bus station, but as time slowly passed, it seemed wiser to go as soon as possible before Ronnie, my husband, knew I was leaving.

I was sad that I didn't get to see Daddy before I left;

I had to tell him goodbye on the phone. My father and I were both crying when I told him that Momma was going to drive us to Orange, Texas, which was half an hour away from my parents' house to catch the bus. We didn't even want to risk going to our local Greyhound station in Louisiana; afraid he might figure things out and catch us there.

I'll never forget that day. It was June 20, 1983, when I left our old painful life. I left our precious dog, Tina, with Momma and boarded the bus with my two little boys and a 38 Derringer in my back pocket for protection. Afraid of what I was leaving and knowing that being on the road with two small children made me a target, I wanted to feel safe. We headed to Austin to lay over with my sister Sheila for a couple of days. We didn't have cell phones at the time, so Mom was going to call ahead to my sister Sheila in Austin and let her know what time I would arrive. We were planning to spend a couple of days with her, since I didn't know when I would see her again. We arrived late that night and got a good night's sleep at my sister's house. The next day, we decided to go to the Springs and have a picnic with the boys. It was so peaceful there, and we just relaxed and had an enjoyable, wonderful day, but it was to be short-lived.

Chapter 7

Starting Over

When we got back to her place, Sheila's husband said that he was getting hang-up calls all day. He would answer, listen, and then someone would hang up. We knew it was Ronnie. I thought I had been so careful, but somehow, he found, or maybe he remembered, her phone number. We decided that I would get on the first bus out the next morning.

I don't remember how long it took to get to my brother's place in Grand Junction, Colorado, but I remember watching out the bus window in awe at snow-capped mountains, in June!! I don't know if the boys realized just what we were doing, but they seemed happy and excited. My son would never have to come into the bathroom again and tell me, "It'll be okay, Mommy," as he patted my leg. (He would find me after a beating just sitting in there). They were finally free to be little boys!

Even when we can't see where we are going or what we are doing, God always has our best interests at heart, and I passionately believe that my parents' prayers were being answered. They were Charismatic Catholics and were strong, spirit-filled prayer warriors.

The timing could not have been better. My brother and his wife were buying a house down the street and moving from the little two-bedroom house they had been renting, and they had already worked it out with his landlord for me to take over the rent for the next couple of months while we figured everything out. My family came together and paid the rent and utilities to get us set up. That first night, the boys and I were settling in. My brother Chris and his wife were just down the street at their new house. Chris told me he would help me get a phone in the next day or two, and I felt relaxed, feeling grateful for my family. After I put the boys to bed, I sat down in a chair to relax and watch TV. The front door was open with just the screen door latched and open to let in a breeze.

I almost jumped out of my skin when someone knocked on the door. I grabbed my derringer as I slowly walked to the door. I looked through the screen door to see a police officer. The officer said, "I don't want to alarm you, ma'am, but we wanted to let you know that we are in the alley behind your house. We had reports of a prowler, so we are checking it out."

Oh, my goodness!! I just knew he had found me. I didn't sleep at all that night and could hardly wait for Chris to show up the next morning. I never heard back from the police, so I don't know if anyone was apprehended in the alley, but at least it wasn't my abuser!!

It was convenient that my brother's ex-wife and their two girls lived in town also, about three blocks behind me, and Chris' new house was about five blocks down the street. As soon as Chris arrived the next morning, I told him what happened, and he immediately gave me a phone. That day, Chris showed me his new house, then he brought us to see my nieces nearby.

The boys and I spent the rest of that day walking around, getting used to our new freedom and becoming familiar with where we lived. I could not help it; I was still fearful, and I was a mess mentally.

I even had a cousin, Danny, who also lived close by, come over with his girlfriend to take me to the Salvation Army to shop. They were so helpful. After explaining that I had moved here with my boys and only our clothes, they gave us food, furniture, dishes, pots and pans, and linens. They encouraged me and really helped me to feel like we were going to be okay. I still couldn't help planning escape routes out of the front and back doors. I didn't want to be caught unaware. Having my cousin Danny there was such a blessing. He took me to the food stamp office to get emergency food stamps and extra help while I was getting my bearings. What a blessing!

Chapter 8

Learning the Hard Way

After getting the house set up, I had to figure out what I was going to do for a job. My youngest niece came over on her bike and stayed with the kids. I used her bike and rode around town, putting in applications for any job I could find.

I was still pretty much an introvert at the time, so I'm sure that I was not making a very good impression when I applied. I was still scared to look people in the eye or even speak very loudly. Therefore, it took me a couple of months to get a job. Thinking back, hindsight being 20/20, it would have been easier if I had been able to complete my schooling back in Louisiana.

Months before, I had started attending a tech school to be an electrician. I had to go five days a week and my sister-in-law offered to watch the boys for me. She had two kids of her own and enjoyed having mine over to play with them. Ronnie was out of work at the time, so he didn't protest too much at first, but when his friends began telling him that I was going to make more than him, it began to bother him. I had already been promised a job making $18.00 an hour to start, which was quite a lot for a female back in the early 80's. He didn't like the fact that I was making friends either, so he made me quit, and I was almost finished.

The school allowed students to work at their own pace, and about five of us were pushing each other. Instead of completing the course in six months, we did it in three. Ronnie made me quit a week before my final exams.

Now, here I was in Colorado with two young boys and no skills, not to mention no self-esteem or confidence. The only thing I knew I could do was be a good mom and maybe wait tables; although, at the time, I really couldn't bring myself to make conversation with anyone. I second-guessed myself because of the abuse and restrictions I had experienced. I was not who I once had been; I had turned into an introvert and was leery of making new friends. The only people I spoke to were people in my family.

Chapter 9

Finding Strength and Closing the Door

Grand Junction, Colorado was a small college town where it was easy to walk everywhere - to the grocery store, the park, and even 'downtown.' It was laid out in a grid, making it easy to navigate once I began to feel more comfortable and safe. The boys and I spent a lot of time at the park during the day because it was free and had a small kiddie pool.

I learned about a domestic abuse program in town, which was within walking distance from where we lived. It offered group sessions, childcare, and counseling for me and the children. Although there is more help available now for victims of domestic abuse, in the 1980s there wasn't much available. People don't realize the emotional prison that battered women are in, with no way out. Even the police were confused as to why women would stay in abusive situations and believed that we must enjoy it. Sadly, some women stay in their emotional prisons their entire lives, and many women die at the hands of their abusive spouses. While I was in Colorado, I heard about a man who had killed his ex-wife and her parents and was hiding in the foothills. I don't know if the authorities ever caught him. It really hit home for me.

As I started attending the group sessions, I heard my own story repeated, again and again. Most abusive relationships start in a similar way. They seem to always begin with beautiful, positive compliments. Most of us agreed that they start out telling us what we want and need to hear. Then, after a while, things change. It seems that people who engage in this sort of behavior find a way to isolate us from family and friends. I could see how past hurts and deep inner pain played a role in creating this opportunity. We agreed that isolating us made us feel unworthy. Past experiences with being hurt and deep inner pain only reinforced the feeling that somehow, we deserved the abuse. Time and time again, I heard the same story. Isolation and abuse were renamed as protection and love, given for our own good. Most of us, for a period of time, believed that all of this was necessary. We believed these spouses to be our heroes, rescuing us from future pain. As anyone might imagine, the emotional abuse was bad enough, but it was only the beginning. The painful abuse starts next: the physical abuse. It may start with a simple slap and then many regrets, accompanied by a lot of tears, with the abuser apologizing and saying it will never happen again. Unless, of course, the abuser decides that you have done something wrong, and the cycle begins again.

By the time a slap turns into a punch, it's easy to become convinced that it's all your fault, that you somehow deserved it, that you made the person do it because that's what they tell you over and over again. For many of us, the control issues seemed like the least of our problems compared to the beatings we had to endure. For many of us, it's the lie that it's for our children's sake that keeps us firmly planted, but children or no children, we just believed the lies.

The women I met in the program were from all over the county and all walks of life - housewives, professional women, average women we see every day and don't know it. There was even a woman who was a deputy sheriff in Texas. I was not alone. Many had done exactly what I had done - they had left many times but went back and forgave their spouses. Why? Because they showed remorse and promised never to do it again. I know I probably left Ronnie half a dozen times before my wake-up call, when he beat our sons.

I believed that children need a father, and I had always believed him when he said they needed him, but I know now that no child deserves a father like that. Although I did not realize it at the time, I saved them from becoming like him. It would have been a generational curse, a lie passed down from the enemy to destroy my children and their children. For Ronnie, this was a cycle that was passed down from his father to him and had probably been passed down for generations. I was now one who would take a stand and break that curse off my boys' lives for the sake of their future family line. Although I didn't know that at the time, I would learn that later. All I knew was that I wanted my boys safe, and I was determined to do whatever it took to achieve that. The only thing I knew at this point was that there was no going back. I could not and would not be abused again, and I would not allow him to hurt my boys ever again.

Chapter 10

Trying to find Closure with Ronnie

It took me about a month to sit down and write a letter to him. In it, I simply said, 'I am not coming back. Period.' No explanation was needed, in my eyes, but I found out years later that he fabricated stories to make himself look like the victim because I had taken his boys from him. Only his younger sister had seen the bruises on them, and she knew the truth.

As I think about his little sister, it's kind of ironic because her ex-husband broke her jaw once and put her in the hospital. Ronnie and his friend went and beat him badly for hitting his sister!

I was still scared that he would find me and come get me, so I mailed the note to my cousin who lived in California. He took it and sent it to Louisiana, and it had a California postmark. So, if he was going to search, it would not be in the state where I was living. Can you imagine being so scared of someone that you went to such extremes? I was afraid for my life. I believed him when he said he would kill me if I ever took his kids from him.

Many years later, I found out that his brother had killed his own wife, because she was leaving him, like I left Ronnie, 'just like Aggie did.' Aggie was my nickname back then. She was going out the door when he struck her on the head with a hammer. They never did find her body, but it was suspected that my ex-husband helped dispose of her in the swamp. He told people that her body would never be found in the swamp. My ex-brother-in-law is serving time in a Texas prison for her murder. He struck a plea bargain when they threatened to charge Ronnie also. If I had any doubts before, I am sure that if I had stayed, Ronnie would have killed me.

About a year after I left, I let down my guard. I tried to sneak back into Louisiana to see my parents. I made the mistake of leaving Mom's house and driving out to where I used to hang out to see some old friends, and a friend of Ronnie's saw me in my dad's truck. He called Ronnie and the next thing I knew,

Ronnie was calling my parents' house, asking to see the boys. I finally agreed to let him come see the boys along with his mother, but he could not leave the house with them.

He came over with his mother to see the boys, and he put on a great act. He was surprisingly dressed up and had gifts for the boys. He spent about an hour playing on the floor with them, trying to make them believe he was this wonderful dad. Unfortunately for him, the boys remembered how mean he was to them and to me. When it was time for them to leave, he tried to convince me to let he and his mom take the boys shopping for new clothes. He refused to pay child support, saying he wasn't going to pay for my 'boyfriends.' Ha! What a laugh. He just wanted an excuse not to pay.

I refused to let him take the boys but told him they could buy the clothes and bring them over in a few days. I left town the next day, knowing he would be trying to hunt me down. I had heard through my old contacts that he was trying to find a way to get me alone. He even used one of my old girlfriends in his scheme. She was living with one of his friends, a guy who was just like him, abusive. Her boyfriend and Ronnie had come up with a plan. She called me and told me Ronnie had bought the boys a horse and was keeping it at her place. She said, "Why don't you bring the boys out to see it? I won't tell him y'all are coming." She lied. I just had an inkling that something was not right and made an excuse not to visit. I found out years later that the men had put her up to it, and the plan was for her to get me and the boys out there, and then they would call Ronnie, who would come take the boys and beat me, or worse. But thank God! I didn't know they were collaborating with Ronnie at the time, but I know God saved me that day, I am sure of it.

After that trip, I would sneak into Louisiana about once a year, but I never left my parents' house. I didn't contact anyone but my family. We would stay hidden, have a good visit with my family, and then leave. But the truth was, I was always on pins and needles the whole time I visited. I was always afraid he, or someone he knew, would find out we were in town. As much as I wanted to, I couldn't even let his mother see them because he lived with her, and I always hated keeping them from their grandmother. I didn't have any more contact with him after that visit. Three years later, I filed for divorce in Colorado. I was able to do it myself with no contact with him. I was able to put an ad in the local paper notifying him of the divorce, and when he did not contest it, it was finalized through the court. It was so easy, it was scary, but necessary. I still could not face him.

It has been many years since my divorce, and I have moved on with my life. I have found happiness and healing, and I have been able to forgive Ronnie for the pain he caused me and my boys. But I will never forget what I went through, and I will always be grateful for the help I received from the Domestic Abuse Program in Grand Junction, Colorado. It was through their support and guidance that I was able to find the strength to start a new life. If you are in an abusive relationship, please don't be afraid to seek help. There are resources available to you, and you deserve to live a life free from fear and abuse.

Chapter 11

Moving On and On and On...

Although I had escaped my nightmare with Ronnie, I still needed inner healing. My desperate need to be loved was still there. I wanted to find love; some deep internal force in me was seeking a sense of belonging. So, I began to go to bars and meet people. But the men were immature, and no one seemed to have any plans for their future. My life had begun to stabilize as I finally got a job at a restaurant, and it seemed that the following year things began to change for the better. A cowboy began to come in during my shift, flirting with me and giving me the attention I was desiring.

I couldn't believe this good-looking cowboy was interested in me! I had felt useless, alone, and unwanted. This was a particularly lonely time. I believed the consensus that I had heard from others that my situation was hopeless because no man would ever want to raise someone else's kids. So, when this good-looking cowboy named John came along, I didn't analyze it, didn't check him out, didn't try to figure out who he was. Once again, I just jumped in with both feet. Luckily, John was a good man, gentle, kind, and attentive. He courted me and moved in with me quickly. He would take the boys and me for rides in the country, exploring Colorado's mountains and lakes on old forest trails. We would go fishing and camping out under the stars. It made it easy to imagine a happy future together.

He told me he was a contractor and he used to build commercial buildings in Denver but was now building residential. The only problem I could find with him at the time was that he was always looking for work but never finding any. So, when the boys were not in school and I had to work, he would take care of them, bathing them, cooking for them, and taking them with him everywhere he went.

Because I was the only one working, we moved a lot, usually to find a cheaper place to rent. One time, we found a small two-bedroom house out in the country, next to a horse pasture that was once a line shack. (That's where cowboys would stay if they got caught in a snowstorm while out checking fences.) It was a cute little place with only a wood-burning stove for heat, and it was cheap. To help pay the rent, we agreed to paint the outside, which meant scraping the old paint off first. Somehow, I ended up getting a paint chip in my eye and had to go to the emergency room. I never knew such pain before. They had to take a tiny drill and cut it out of my cornea. Then, I was put on painkillers and was told my eye would have to heal itself. I spent the next two weeks on the couch, unable to do anything because of the pain, and John took care of me and the boys and finished the house painting. My boys, Smokey and Zach, loved that little house out in the country, especially the horses that would come to the fence to be petted. One Appaloosa especially loved my youngest son, Zach, and would come running to the fence whenever Zach would go outside. Zach named him Spots, even though he wasn't our horse, and he cried when we had to move a few months later. Unfortunately, after we painted the house, the landlord wanted more rent, which we didn't have enough income for, so we were moving again. Zach was crushed, and I promised him I would get him a horse of his own one day. He is grown now and, until this day, he still reminds me of that promise.

Not long after moving into an apartment, a former next-door neighbor and friend, Diane, from when I had first arrived in Colorado, contacted me. Diane and her husband, and their two girls, had moved to Austin, Texas for work. Mark was in construction, and said business was booming, and he encouraged us to move there. John and I decided to move to Austin, Texas, and I would go first to stay with them for a couple of weeks, and get things set up, while he took care of loose ends in Colorado. So, on the road again, the boys and I packed up what we could in my little car and left for the hill country. Little did I know that, for John, this was all a test.

When I got to Diane's, I immediately got the ball in motion. I got the boys enrolled in the same school as her girls and found a job at a supermarket as a cashier. I had only been there for a couple of weeks when John called me and told me it was time to come home. I said, "What are you talking about? I just got things set up, and I will start work soon." He said he only sent me there because he thought I needed a break, but he wanted me to come back. As I said, he was "testing" me to see if I would come back. So, feeling like a fool, I packed up the car and the boys and moved back. Ignoring the huge red flag, and the mind games that John was playing, I realize now that I wasn't the only one who was broken in this relationship!

To make matters worse, when we got back to Colorado, after only a couple of months, he announced that we were moving to Arizona. We moved around from town to town for a couple of months at a time, seeking work, and to this day, I don't know how we had the funds to do all the moving we did. We were in Flagstaff for a bit, then Cottonwood, then Camp

Verde, and finally in Apache Junction. My kids were in 6 different schools in 6 months, we were living like vagabonds.

We finally caught a break in Apache Junction, where John met a man who wanted us to build houses for him. So, for the next six months, that's what we did. I helped by learning everything I could in carpentry work. I helped with building walls, all the way up to roofing. I enjoyed it more than waitress work, but sadly, after things dried up, I had to go back to waiting tables to put food on the table. But then we caught a break, and about six months later, we landed a job building a custom house at the base of Superstition Mountain.

I thought we had finally made it. It took us about eight months to build because he and I did everything but plumbing, concrete, and electric. The couple we were building the house for really loved the house, and I was sure more jobs would come in, but as soon as it was done, things shifted. John sent me to Louisiana to visit my parents; a vacation, he said.

I drove to Louisiana in my car and spent two weeks with my parents, but my car broke down in a big way, and the car was not able to make the trip back. I had to fly back to Arizona with two young boys and my small dog, Tina, in tow.

On the trip back, something amazing happened. John told me that he had bought a place for us in the mountains in a little town called Clay Springs, just outside of Show Low, Arizona. When we were due to get back, we were planning on driving up the mountain that night, but because of a delay in our flight, we got stuck in the Denver airport for five hours.

We didn't arrive in Arizona until 9 p.m. at night and decided to get a hotel room for the night instead of driving up a winding mountain road in the dark. And what wisdom that turned out to be. When John backed the truck up to the door of our room to unload the bags for the night, the steering column broke on our truck. I am certain that God had intervened in the delay so that we were saved from going off the side of the mountain that night.

I believed in God, but I wasn't reading the Word of God. My Mom always prayed for me, and I know now, looking back, that God was protecting us and watching over us every step of the way.

We got the truck fixed the next day, and in a snowstorm, we made it up to the trailer he had purchased. The only problem was we were without propane gas for heat for two days. One more thing to be thankful to God for, an electric blanket that kept us all warm until the propane company could get up the mountain to us.

Hope glimmered in my heart, as it was a nice trailer on an acre of land in a quaint little square-mile town. I do literally mean a square mile. It was laid out with a schoolhouse down one road, a post office a mile down the next road, and a general store up the next square mile. With houses off the different roads. My boys can honestly say they had to walk a mile to school in the snow because there was no bus. But we did have a nice little hill for sledding on our land, and we all played in the snow.

As we got acquainted with our little town, I began to volunteer at the school. The boys were in first and second grade by now, and it was a small one-room schoolhouse, so volunteers were always needed and appreciated. I was meeting other Moms at school and even doing things outside of school with them like helping with canning at a neighbor's house.

But John was out of work again, and before the month was out, he began talking about work in Virginia. He was planning to go by himself and leave us in Arizona for the time being. Looking back, I don't think he planned on us following him.

He left, and I had to get a job at the supermarket in the next town. I had to get the boys to daycare because of work and drive about 30 minutes each way. What I didn't know at the time was that my youngest son struggled with dyslexia and needed help to read. Unfortunately, when I had to quit helping the others at the school, they quit helping me, and we got shunned. They were a tight-knit Mormon community, and if you were not part of the community, then you were not part of their inner circle. They shunned me. What I found out was that women are not allowed to work outside of the home. If I had agreed to learn and practice their beliefs, they would have taken care of us, but that was not where I wanted to be, so I quickly made plans to give up the trailer and drive out to Virginia and meet up with John.

He got us an apartment before we arrived, and we walked away from the place in Arizona. We lived there for a year, with me working as a waitress in a restaurant when he wasn't working, which oddly enough came about every six months. We were establishing a pattern of jumping up and leaving every six months.

Once, my parents came to visit for Smokey's birthday. We had a little family time, decorated a cake. It was hard moving every 6 months. I was hoping at some point we could settle down.

Although we had a visit from my parents, which helped me feel a little more stable, I never had enough time to establish myself. Just when we would get established, John would get up and move us again.

Another move, this time we got a call from John's mom who lived in Rifle, Colorado. She asked John to come home and take care of her. She had been diagnosed with breast cancer and needed help to go through chemotherapy. We picked up our lives once again and moved back to Colorado.

John was the youngest of four children and the only one who lived out of state, but for one reason or another, he was the only one who was willing and able to help. We found out later that she had received these diagnoses 5 years ago but waited till she was old enough for Medicare to do anything.

We moved in with her to help, and she began chemotherapy. John, wanting his mother to witness him getting married, asked me to marry him, and I said yes. I honestly thought, because of that, this marriage would be forever.

Those years had been one big test for John! He later confessed to me that he never wanted to get married because his last girlfriend had cheated on him and taken half of everything he had. Of course, now I realize that was only one side of the story. They had lived together for several years, and she had contributed to the relationship by helping him run his business as a commercial contractor but did not stick it out with his ups and downs. Because I had stayed with him through all the difficulties for the last couple of years,

I had passed his 'test.' I hadn't put it together in my head yet, but that is why he worked six months and then couldn't find anything the next six months. He was seeing if I would stick around. He liked to play mind games.

After a couple of months, his mother was admitted to the hospital in Vail, Colorado, which was about an hour away. John couldn't handle sitting with her in the hospital every day, so I became the one who sat with her daily from 9 a.m. to 9 p.m. every day for three weeks. I would take a break and go home for a day and then return. She had a cabin in Minturn, which was ten minutes away from the hospital, so I stayed there a week at a time while my kids stayed with John.

Unfortunately, his mother continued to get worse. The chemo wasn't working, and she was getting weaker and weaker. As I was going home at the end of the third week, she passed away, and John made final arrangements.

His mother being sick and dying took its toll on our relationship in so many ways. To start with, she had changed her will when we agreed to come take care of her. She cut the other three siblings out of her will completely and left everything to John, which turned out to be a lot more than we expected. She lived like a pauper on a small monthly social security check, but we located five other bank accounts with almost

$10,000 dollars each and land and property in Colorado and Arizona, not to mention the large apartment that had been converted from a church. She also had another apartment full of items that came from a previous import/export shop, where she used to have an extensive doll collection and just tons of stuff we had to go through.

John didn't feel right about keeping everything, so we set out to inventory her items from the shop, which took almost six months with the two of us working on it from daylight to dark, seven days a week. We had garage sales every other weekend and gave things to his brothers and sister, including her car and the doll collection to his only niece. After all was taken care of, John decided to give them each some of the money and gave his sister the entire contents of the store, which was quite extensive: ivory from India, turquoise jewelry from Arizona Indian reservations, and wooden pottery, jewelry, and knick-knacks from all over the world. I am sure it was worth thousands of dollars, but John was tired and continually being harassed by his siblings, and I think he just wanted to be done with all of it. Once they got what they wanted, they just kind of faded away.

John and I decided to move back to Arizona while he was still grieving her passing. John started studying astrology and got heavy into astrological mapping. He told me that he had promised his mother he would always be close to her, and now that he was no longer bound by that promise, we could live anywhere we wanted. As he began to study, he gave me a choice of living in Austin or Houston, Texas. I chose Houston because it was halfway between my parents' house in Louisiana and my sister in Austin. Little did I know that it was the beginning of the end.

It was early May in 1990 and John gave me $1,500.00 to move to Houston and get things set up. It sounded like a lot of money back then, but we were looking for a house with a fenced-in yard for our dogs. I was driving back and forth from my parents' house every day, a two-hour drive, searching for a house and a job. When I thought I had found a good house and added up all the deposits for the house and utilities, I knew I needed more money. John said he would not send any more money, that I would have to make it work. So, back to the search for a stable home.

I had a friend who lived on the outskirts of Houston, and I stayed with her and her family for a few days to regroup. I focused my efforts on getting a job. At that point, I had secured two jobs waiting tables. I was able to secure an apartment on a six-month lease. As soon as I did, I called John and told him. He seemed okay with it, then a week later, as I was moving in, he called me and told me it was time to move back to Arizona.

My frustration level hit an all-time high when, under the promise of settling down, I had just spent two months searching for a place for my family, totally believing that we were starting over in a new place. When John called and told me that he had just signed a six-month lease on an apartment, he expected me to pack up the boys and cancel everything I had done and move back with him to Arizona.

I had a major decision to make. I had just finished dealing with his mother's death and liquidating her estate, going to Houston, and searching for a place. I had just signed a lease on an apartment and was reluctant to uproot my boys once again. I had the opportunity to live closer to my parents who were not getting any younger. I pondered what to do, and an opportunity to go to work for the apartment complex as a leasing agent popped up. I had known others in my past that had worked as leasing agents and was really excited about the chance to change my career path from being a waitress. My choice was really to remain stable or go back to mind games and moving constantly.

There were also all the issues and constant diffi-culties, and the mind games John had been playing since I met him. I began to have questions. Why was he always out of work every six months, depending on me to support us every six months? And why was it so difficult to settle down in one place? The boys and

I loved the small town where his mom lived and had a totally paid for house to live in. Things just didn't add up anymore and after talking extensively to my parents, I decided to stay in Texas, close to family, get a new career and not uproot my boys. When I told John he needed to move here, he got upset and cut off all communication. Two months later I got divorce papers in the mail. Sometimes we see more clearly, looking back, hindsight truly is 20/20! There were issues there I didn't know about, like his involvement in the occult activities, namely astrology. He was all over the place. At one point he talked me into studying with some Jehovah Witnesses, and after about six months, I just couldn't agree with what they were saying.

He seemed to have a lack of identity, and at one point claimed to be an undercover narcotics agent when we first met, and he was now in the process of writing a book about it. He did write the book, which was more of a manual, but nothing ever came of it. As I said before, things were not what they seemed. I was tired of the mind games and felt like I was paying for all his past relationship mistakes. According to him, all the women in his life had always messed him over, including his mom. It was more than I could overcome.

So, this time I decided it was time to move on and start fresh once again. I still could not openly go to Louisiana because of my ex-husband, Ronnie, but it had been years since there was any contact, and I was feeling safe where I was.

Reflection

In thinking about John and his ups and downs, always testing me and moving us every six months, it became clearer to me now that I am Christian, that John and I were not basing our identity or worth in Christ. He was not seeking the Lord for a relationship with him nor asking for God's wisdom for direction in his decisions. The bible speaks of this problem in the book of James.

James 1:5 KJV

5If any of you lack wisdom, let him ask of God, that giveth to all men liberally, and upbraideth not; and it shall be given him. 6But let him ask in faith, nothing wavering. For he that wavereth is like a wave of the sea driven with the wind and tossed. 7For let not that man think that he shall receive any thing of the Lord. 8A double minded man is unstable in all of his ways.

Chapter 12

Love IS

John and I divorced. The kids and I had been off Ronnie's radar for nearly sixteen years. When I heard that Ronnie had died, I went to the funeral and found out that a former acquaintance of mine had become his girlfriend for the past fifteen years. Oddly enough, I had at one point suspected them of having an affair. I found out that she had been hospitalized numerous times and probably had almost every bone in her body broken at one time or another by him. When I asked her why she stayed, she said, 'I loved him.'

Hearing of this abuse happening to someone else made my spirit shout! "That is not love! It might be lust, or need, or dependence, but it is not love, on either side!"

Reflection

After all of these years my relationship with God, who is love, had taught me the difference between God's real love, and even real love we show one another and what the difference was. I praise God for that.

The Bible says in 1 Corinthians 13: 4-7:

"Love suffers long and is kind; love does not envy; love does not parade itself, is not puffed up; does not behave rudely, does not seek its own, is not provoked, thinks no evil; does not rejoice in iniquity, but rejoices in the truth; bears all things, believes all things, hopes all things, endures all things."

Love is not selfish or self-centered. When you love someone, you want the best for them. You put their needs above yours. Any mom will tell you this is true. We may not always be perfect or even correct but we want to do what we feel is best for our children. We want to protect them with everything we have, every-thing in us, like a momma bear protecting her cubs. We want to give them the world and certainly every advantage to conquer their world. That is love as I see it.

Chapter 13

When Perception Believed Becomes Reality Lived

Looking back, I wondered how I had become the woman who could let herself be abused. Where did she come from? I asked myself, "How did I get here?" All I ever wanted was to be loved, to have a family with a loving husband and children. I never wanted a career; I just wanted to be a mom and wife. I had always wanted children, always loved being with them and taking care of them. I started babysitting when I was thirteen and enjoyed every minute of it. I even had a dream of having twenty kids! Can you imagine that? I had a friend growing up who had twelve siblings, and I thought that was the best thing ever.

Even though I was raised in a Catholic home, going to Catholic schools, and had experienced religion, I did not have a sense of who I truly was in God. All my searching came from my desire to feel loved. My perception at the time was that I was never "good enough" or "smart enough." My grades in school were average because I stopped trying. Even when I studied, I could never make it past a grade of "C." I was always told I was stupid, so I stopped putting forth the effort. And pretty? Even if I was, I did not know it; I was told I was ugly, repeatedly! By whom? My little brother, and he was family. In my mind, I thought, "Well, if he is my family, he ought to know, right?" It might have been dismissed as kid's banter, but the real problem was that no one ever corrected him or said to me that what he was saying was not true. The perception that he was an authority, and that no one disagreed, led to my perception that this was true. In fact, these were lies that came from Satan himself who used my little brother's ignorance to deliver them. The problem was that I believed the lies. I let the lies of the enemy sink deep into my heart and soul. If anyone says words don't hurt, that's a lie. Words can kill your desires, your dreams, and damage your soul. I was always in the shadow of my younger brother. Let me pause here and go back to my younger years, starting with birthdays.

My birthday is exactly a week before Christmas, so the focus was always on Christmas. I might have been able to deal with being told, "Your birthday is too close to Christmas, so we'll just give it all in one," but my little brother had it different. Mike's birthday was a month earlier in November and he always had a birthday. He always had a special celebration with cake and ice cream and friends over for a party. The only party I ever had was one I gave myself when I turned sixteen. It was just a slumber party for my girlfriends from school, but my brother ruined that before the end of the night.

At that time, we had a small room next to our trailer that had been converted into a bedroom. My middle brother had just gotten married and moved out of it. I went to my mom and asked her for that room, and she said, "Yes." I spent the entire day cleaning it and getting ready for my slumber party. I was so excited! I would have my own space, outside! Before everyone arrived, my little brother asked me what I was doing. I told him I was cleaning my room and he went straight to Mom and convinced her to let him have the room instead of me. I was allowed to have my slumber party that night, but then he would get the room as his bedroom. I couldn't believe what was happening! After she had told me it was mine, and I had spent the entire day cleaning and scrubbing that room, he came in and took it from me. When I asked her why, she told me, "I don't think it is a good idea. After all, your cousin got his girlfriend pregnant in that room, and now your brother has gotten his girlfriend pregnant in the same room."

"Mom," I argued, "I am not going to get pregnant or have sex in there. I am a virgin, and I am going to stay that way until I get married. Please believe me, trust me." She didn't listen to me or believe me, and my brother got the room anyway. And by the way, he ended up getting his girlfriend pregnant in that same room a few years later!

So, here I was, hurt again by the favoritism. It didn't matter what I did or said; I was coming in second to him, again. I always did, and it hurt me deeply. They say parents shouldn't have favorites, but I felt like mine did. I always felt that he was the kid they wanted, but I was just there. If Momma fixed something for supper that he didn't want, she would fix him something else! He never had to clean up after himself, do dishes, or any chores in the house. He didn't clean his room, do laundry, or anything! I, on the other hand, had to clean the kitchen at night and clean the whole house on Saturday before I could do anything or go anywhere. I was required to dust, sweep, mop, clean the bathroom, and even do the laundry. Was it because I was the only girl in the house or just because it was me? I felt like a maid and couldn't wait to leave.

I wanted to get my driver's license, but Momma said I had to go through driver's education at school. I finally got it at seventeen but was not allowed to even start the family car for church on Sundays. In the meantime, one of the ladies I babysat for would take me and my girlfriend out in her car on the weekends and let us drive her around. She taught us both how to drive her car with a standard transmission. Daddy taught my brother how to drive his truck and let him help with trash pick-up in the trailer park. We had bought a trailer park from Mom's cousin, and it was our responsibility to take all the trash to the dump. My brother was only fourteen at the time, not old enough to get a license, but Daddy needed his help, so he taught him how to drive. I decided to get a job, but it was a catch-22 situation. I couldn't go to work because I didn't have a car, and I couldn't get a car because I didn't have a job or money. I thought if I got a job, Momma would help me get to it, but she refused and told me to figure it out. When I asked if she would help me get a car, she said, "No, I made that mistake with the older kids." I don't know what she meant by that, except they gained freedom and left home, which of course they each did as soon as they graduated from high school.

I was a junior in high school, and I began smoking pot, trying to dull the pain I felt from the rejection I lived with. I would also drink whenever I could get my hands on some wine, and that was easy back then. The convenience stores didn't check IDs, and the legal drinking age in Louisiana was eighteen. I passed the "looking the age" test! Or maybe I just acted like I knew what I was doing! Smoking pot and drinking would become a thorn in my side, ultimately costing me relationships and opportunities.

Reflection

I was never good enough, I never felt loved or loveable because of my childhood. I used to have the attitude, "if they don't like me the way I am, that's their problem." The down-deep problem was I didn't like me! I did not know the truth that God genuinely loved me so much that he gave his son, Jesus on the cross to set me free from all these feelings of being unloved and unworthy. I was the middle child in my family, fourth in line behind three older siblings that had made a lot of mistakes and one younger sibling. My parents made decisions based on the knowledge and tools they had at the time. With Gods help and transformation of my thought process I was able to forgive my mother, father, and brother and move on in my life.

Chapter 14

A Way Out

The summer prior to my senior year, I had been babysitting for a genuinely nice couple, Debbie and Butch, who had two boys. I had confided in Debbie and poured out my heart. When they asked me to move to Texas with them to help start a "Repo" business, I jumped at the chance. I would babysit as needed and use my accounting skills, which I had learned in school, to help as needed in their business. We were able to convince my mom that it was a fantastic opportunity and she let me go. I would have to start public school in Beaumont, Texas for my senior year. We went to Beaumont as planned, and I started high school, but it didn't work out as I had imagined. They would not give me credit for two of my history classes and were requiring me to take three history classes to graduate. I hated history and knew I could not pass all three classes. After trying for two weeks to straighten it out, and becoming frustrated, I just gave up. I talked to Debbie about it, and we decided that my best option at this point was to quit and go to work. We called my mom and she agreed. Debbie was willing to take me back and forth to work until I could save for a car. I began working for Walgreens as a "cosmetologist" and things were going well. I enjoyed my job, and we were all settling into a comfortable routine. When I wasn't working, I helped around the apartment and we would go with Butch to repo cars, which was fun, though sometimes scary. One night, Debbie and I had to hide in a ditch when someone tried to shoot us for repossessing his car!

A couple of weeks after I started my job, I got a phone call from my little brother. He wanted to give me some exciting news! "Mom bought me a car!" he said. I was speechless! Tears coursed down my face. I handed the phone to Debbie. I went to my room and cried. I was heartbroken. I had begged her to help me, and now, I hadn't even been gone a month, and she had bought him a car. I was beyond hurt. I felt rejected once again and couldn't wrap my mind around it. Did she hate me? Had I done something wrong? Had I not done something she wanted me to do? I knew my brother wasn't working. He was only fifteen and didn't have his license yet. My parents had not even told him to take driver's ed like I was told to in order to drive. I felt like my mom was doing all of this to hurt me. I thought, "Am I such a bad person? I did everything she asked when I lived there. I obeyed my curfews, was always home on time, and didn't even date until I turned seventeen." I couldn't speak to either of them for weeks. I was broken-hearted and rejected once again.

I continued to work my job and tried to be a help to Debbie as much as I could, but I was truly heartbroken. I was beyond broken; my heart was shattered. I loved my mom and could not understand why she didn't like me, or so I thought. Why would she deny me help and then turn around and do it for my little brother, once again? I felt so rejected and hurt. At that point, I looked for ways that I thought might dull the pain, so I started smoking pot again. I continued to work, but one day, a couple of months later, I came home to Butch and Debbie's, and it was announced that Butch was promptly bringing me home to my parents that day! Why? Because Debbie had found out that I was smoking pot and there was no discussion, no debate, and no second chances. Debbie had decided to kick me out and had already called my mom and arranged to bring me home. I was told, "Pack your bags; you're going to have to leave. I know you are smoking pot, and I have already let your mother know we are bringing you home." I had no argument with her, and her husband drove me home in silence to my parents' house in Louisiana. Heartbroken again because the one person I had confided in had turned her back on me, too. Now I was back where I started, with no chance to even talk about it! I didn't smoke very often; I didn't even know anyone in town, but a friend would mail me a joint or two occasionally. I think I had only had two the whole time I was living with Debbie. The only reason she knew was because I had started dating her brother, and I had tried to get him to smoke with me. When we broke up, he told her. The sad part for me was that if she had only talked to me about it and told me to quit, I would have. Unfortunately, the way it played out, I just experienced one more rejection to add to many others I had already experienced in my young life. My thoughts raced, and I thought, "Am I that bad of a person? Am I so unlovable? I thought I was a decent human being. I don't lie, cheat, or steal. I am loving and honest and would help anyone who needs it. Why doesn't anyone love me? All I have ever wanted was to be loved!" And now I was back to square one - back at my mom's house where I was told that I was ugly and stupid!

Reflection

The root of rejection was planted so deep in my young life that hearing that my brother had been given what I thought I deserved made me feel that much more rejected. I sought out ways to cope and dull the pain, through superficial relationships and drugs. The lie was that somehow my mother loved me less than my brother, that she did not see what I was attempting to do right or the sacrifices I was making. The truth was something else though. The perspective that I could never have until becoming a parent myself was that my mother was working with the tools she had and doing her best to protect me although I could not understand it at the time. Was she right, was she wrong? I do not know. All I know is that the triggers that sent me into that downward spiral back to pot and superficial relationships were rooted in my own lack of identity in Christ. The bible says that I have great worth, that I am made in the image of God, that my worth is not based on the opinions of others but on God's opinion of me. You and I have such a steep price tag that Jesus Christ paid for it with his life willingly, to bring us home.

At this time of my life, I got all of my self-worth from what others said and thought about me, all of my love from relationships with men. I was looking for God's true love but had instead found counterfeits.

We are fearfully and wonderfully made (Psalm 139:14) We are free of the past and free to live life to the fullest!

1 PETER 3:3-4 ESV
Do not let your adorning be external—the braiding of hair and the putting on of gold jewelry, or the clothing you wear— but let your adorning be the hidden person of the heart with the imperishable beauty of a gentle and quiet spirit, which in God's sight is very precious.

Chapter 15

Acceptance

Back at home from Debbie's, I needed to start over. I was nearly eighteen and had gone job hunting. I found a small local bar not far from my parents' trailer park and, after talking to the owner, got a job on the spot. I had never been a bartender, but he assured me it was easy, and we never got any "fancy" drink orders. He worked with me the first few hours and then left me with the keys, promising to come help close, but he didn't and that was the way it was from then on. I would arrive at 4:00 p.m., he would leave, and I would close the bar.

Being in a bar, I picked up some new skills. I learned to play pool like a pro from the pool sharks who spent most of their days there. Unfortunately, they also taught me to drink hard liquor, one shot at a time! The bar life became my life, and the patrons there became my new family. When I wasn't working, I went there. It was the place I was trusted, welcomed, and accepted, unlike at home. I was encouraged to drink because the bar made money when customers bought me drinks. When word got out amongst friends that I was working there, people I knew came in and we would have a full bar most weekends. I stayed busy, but I was truly still lonely.

I began once again looking for love in all the wrong places, and soon it found me. I met Charles while I was working one night, and he swept me off my feet. He was a few years older, good-looking, charming, and had a heavy Italian accent. He said everything I wanted to hear. He promised to take me away, give me a great life in Boston, Massachusetts, and love me forever. He wanted to go to Las Vegas to get married, and I jumped at the opportunity to get away from my life! I would give him my heart, and he would give me a new life!

I knew him for only three days, and I said, "Yes!" We went to my parents together and convinced them we had known each other for a while. Charles asked their permission to take me away and marry me. We never told them that we had only known each other for three days; we lied, and they said, "Okay!" To this day, I don't know why it was so easy to convince them. I searched in my heart for an underlying reason and was determined to believe that it was a way for them to not have to pay for a wedding. The truth is that I still do not know.

This was not my first engagement; I had been engaged once before, only a year earlier, and had called it off two days before the bridal shower! He was a good ole country boy who lived with his parents in my parents' trailer park. We got along great, liked the same things, went out often, and had a great time together. We dated for a year and a half, and I had even made my wedding dress when I was a junior in high school. I got cold feet and ran from the one who could and would have loved me with everything he had! But, again, I was not following God and was so lost. I was making stupid decisions, mostly based on emotions, and here I was doing it again, leaving home with a man who was really a stranger. I barely knew his name. I just took his word for everything he said.

We drove to Vegas, taking us three days to get there. I was not scared or nervous; we were having fun and getting to know each other. He was a gentleman the whole time and we had separate hotel rooms when we would stop for the night. I had told him I had planned on being a virgin on my wedding night, and he showed me honor and respect. I had no idea what the future would hold, but I had high hopes and was believing it would be good.

It was crazy, stupid on my part; anything could

have happened. He could have been with a serial killer or planning to sell me into a sex trafficking ring. I was so naive. All I could think about was getting away forever. I was looking forward to being a wife and mother. I so desperately wanted and needed to be loved. Surprisingly, Charles and I got married in a little chapel in Vegas and stayed in town for a few days. We saw a couple of live shows and then headed back across the U.S. When we got to Tennessee, he put me on a plane to go home for a few days because he had to take care of an emergency. He didn't tell me what it was, and after only a week and a half, I was back at my parents' house.

My fairytale started to fade even more when I didn't hear from him when I got home, but I did get a personal visit from the FBI about two weeks later! Apparently, my "new husband" and three other men had robbed a bank in Boston. They found my information in the pocket of his jacket, which he left in the "get-away car"! I know it sounds bizarre, but it's the truth. This gives a whole new meaning to the scripture that says the truth shall set you free. The FBI wanted to know what I knew, and if I had heard from him. I had not, and I began to spiral down emotionally from there. I became even more lost and desperate if that was possible.

After this fiasco, I was a mess, as you can imagine. So, after a couple of months at home, I got involved with my neighbor, who was eight years older, and whom I had known for years. He was my best friend's older brother, who had taken us camping when we were younger. He was home on leave from prison due to drug charges and had just been cheated on by his ex. We sympathized with each other, and our friendship turned into something more. He wanted me to wait for him to get out of prison in a few months, and I said I would.

I convinced myself that I was in love, but I had no idea what true love felt like. I didn't know how to give it or receive it. I went back to what I knew, working at the bar, and waited for Ernest to come home. We wrote to each other constantly, and I prepared for his homecoming. He finally came home, and for three years we lived together, doing something I had sworn to myself I would never do: live in sin, that is, live unmarried with a man. Gone were the hopes and dreams of a young girl; I didn't care. I was trying to mold myself into what he wanted, and I became heavily involved in drugs, even shooting up. I hated needles and had sworn I would never do that either!

My whole life revolved around being 'loved', and once again my search for true love was taking me down roads I was never meant to take. I look back at that season in my life now and see how low I had sunk to please a man to get the love I longed for to fulfill me. I had always dreamed of being a wife and mother, but that did not fit into his plans. He said he never wanted to get married, so I lied to please him and said the same.

I would cook for him and clean for him and do what I could to make him happy. When we were out of money, I would even steal food or clothes for him, all to please him when he was not working and contributing. I went to work as a waitress, bringing home my tips so he could go out with 'the guys'. I was devoted and gave everything, even my identity, my hopes, and my dreams.

Then the unthinkable happened: he cheated on me. For a couple of weeks, I felt like something was wrong, and when I confronted him about it, he confirmed my suspicions. He had been taking someone else out on the tip money I was making. It was devastating.

I had put my life in his hands, and he had crushed it. I felt I was reaping what I had sown in the past. I felt undeserving of his faithfulness because, the truth be told, I had cheated years earlier on him after we had first gotten together. I had asked for his forgiveness, and we stayed together.

I told myself that it was never going to be a forever relationship because I had broken the trust, and years of my faithfulness had not gotten it back. Some people might call it karma, but the Bible calls it reaping and sowing, a principle of the kingdom of God.

Galatians 6:7-8 says:

"Be not deceived, God is not mocked, for whatsoever a man soweth, that shall he also reap. For he that soweth to his flesh shall of the flesh reap corruption, but he that soweth to the Spirit shall of the Spirit reap life everlasting."

Chapter 16

Saved

Reeling from a broken heart, I headed to the nearest convenience store looking for something to save me from the pain. I went in and got a fifth of Boone's Farm strawberry wine, my go-to mood enhancer. I drove to the convention center to sit by the lake in solitude. After drinking about half the bottle, the alcohol made me feel bold, a little bit brave, and I didn't care so much or think of the consequences.

I got out of the car to take a walk on the Seawall and I met a guy. He seemed nice enough and we began talking about anything and everything. We talked for hours. His name was Steven, and he lived by himself in town. We reluctantly said goodbye, exchanged phone numbers, and parted company for the night. We began to spend hours talking on the phone and eventually began to date.

After a couple of weeks, he invited me to church, and I said yes. The church was in a little storefront on Main Street. It was a small congregation, and the pastor and his wife were young and down to earth. but full of passion. I'd never heard anything like this. God loves me? I didn't feel like anyone loved me, even my family just kind of tolerated me, but love? I didn't think I knew what that was.

As I sat listening to him preach about God's sacrifice for me, my heart began to fill with love and acceptance, knowing that God truly cared about me and for me. I believed this preacher and wanted to hear more. I began to get hungry for this love. When church was over, I went back to Steven's house with him, and we began to read the Bible together.

The Word of God began to become real to me for the first time in my life. I had grown up in a Catholic house, going to church every Sunday and going to Catholic school all my life, but never got anything out of it. We were told not to read the Bible because we wouldn't understand it. That big Bible on the coffee table? It was just for show. I had always been an avid reader, but this was different. I wanted to know everything. I was consumed with learning what the Bible said about Jesus.

The next weekend, I gave my life to the Lord, and

when the preacher asked if I wanted to receive the baptism of the Holy Spirit, I said that I wanted everything God had for me. I received the baptism with the evidence of tongues immediately. I was immediately changed. I was totally filled with God's love. I was in love with God and Jesus.

There was a huge move of the Holy Spirit in the Catholic Church at this time, and my parents both got involved. They got saved and filled with the Holy Spirit and got a hunger for more of God. Mom started going to meetings and learning with her new saved friends, and she found out about Women's Aglow, and that's how I got introduced to Aglow. Mom brought me to a meeting where the speaker was prophesying to people, and I got a hunger for the gift of prophecy. They said I could have it too and prayed for me to receive the gift of prophecy. I received it immediately along with the gift of interpretation and diverse tongues (according to 1 Cor. 12).

It was an exciting time for us. Mom, Dad, and I would sit around the kitchen table and pray in tongues and prophecy to each other. We began to record the prophecies and transcribe them and filled up a couple of notebooks. It became a nightly thing for us.

We were all learning how to walk in the Spirit together, and differences were put aside as we heard from God. God was revealing the future, my future, and to tell the truth, it scared me. I never saw myself as much of anything and the things God was showing us was more than I could take in or comprehend.

I was still broken and rejected and didn't know how to accept it. I didn't know how to get healed, didn't realize I needed to be healed. I just thought this was the hand I was dealt and had to accept it. Steven asked me to marry him, and I said yes. Then he began talking about going around the world to spread the gospel together. I agreed, but inside I struggled and couldn't see it.

I could not accept that God really wanted me, so I backslid, and I ran. Somewhere inside me I still was lost in my identity, not feeling worthy of all God had for me, despite all that I had experienced with God.

But God never gave up on me and continued to love me and protect me, even during my sin and self-destruction. Again, I thank God for praying parents, who never gave up either. I can remember them kneeling by their bed together even when we were kids, praying for me and my four siblings.

That's what I knew, that's where I was comfortable and felt acceptance, even if it was short-lived moments of happiness. I immersed myself in a life of forgetting the pain of my mistakes and past hurts and living in the moment, more like living from one high to the next.

I know now that this is not who God created me to be. He wants me to know that I am loved, forgiven, accepted, and worthy. He wants me to walk in peace, love, and a sound mind. He wants to prepare me for all that he has for me, which is good by the way. However, the lie of the enemy won a temporary battle, but not the war.

Chapter 17

Reading the Instructions

If only we had a set of detailed instructions to guide us through life. If we only had text, we could refer to it.

As a child, I was raised Catholic and had gone to Mass every Sunday and attended Catholic schools all my life, but I did not truly know God or His Word. I knew 'about' Him, and I had heard some of the stories in the Bible, but that's all they were to me, just stories and history.

I was raised in the 1960s and 1970s, during which time it was not promoted in the Catholic Church to study the Bible independently. We were told in the Catholic Church not to read the Bible because we wouldn't be able to understand it for ourselves. The sad part is that I really didn't understand the Mass performed in the Catholic church service, because it was performed mostly in Latin! Nevertheless, we always went as a family and never missed a church service. The only Bible we had at home was the big coffee table Bible kept where people could see it! In religion class, we had religion books! I couldn't even tell you what they said - that's how much they meant to me!

And I have always been an avid reader; I love to read! I always had a book in my hand, I just didn't know the Bible was the best book in the world to read! I highly recommend it. It has everything in it!

It's not just God's love story to us, but it tells us about our history from the beginning, all the way to the end of the ages. The Bible tells the stories of loving husbands and unfaithful lovers like Haggai and his wife, and shows what redemptive love looks like. It tells of heroes and heroines and a future that sounds like science fiction!

The Bible tells the story of Ruth, who went through great hardship and loss, came into a new land, and started over. Through her faithfulness to God and family, God redeemed her, leading her to her one true love. The Bible is the place where you find God's plan for redemption for you yourself and for each one of us, through His only begotten son, Jesus.

If we read God's Word, study it, by ourselves and with others, it will enrich our lives, guide us, and keep us. I didn't know there was a moral code, or guidelines to live by! Some people call it by an acronym --

B --Basic
I -- Instructions
B -- Before
L -- Leaving
E – Earth

And that's exactly what it is! I used to get frustrated when I asked what His will was for me, and all I got was, "It's in the Word," and this is so true! It may not say, "Agnes, I want you to be a missionary or a doctor, or a nurse," but it does say, "I want you to follow me and spread my Word to the nations" (Mark 16:16-19).

I knew there was a Savior who died, but I didn't know about His life, or that He died for me! I didn't know that He had a plan from the beginning of time, and it's all in His story, the Word of God. I didn't know that I was searching for the love of a Father and the love of a Savior, like so many are!

These days, in 2023, there are so many resources available to anyone who is searching. There are internet searches, where you can find a youth group or a Bible study, online or in-person. There are some good, Bible-based churches, sometimes called "Word Churches." You can talk about God with others on social media and not be afraid to reach out.

Back then, when I was a teenager, I didn't know where to turn. I had no youth group to turn to, no pastor that could relate, no cell phone or internet to search. I was lost in my own pain and didn't know any way out! But God had given me a praying mother and father who never gave up on me. Years later, in the 90s, after I was truly saved and made the decision to follow God and never give up, I found a God that had never given up on me, either. He was there.

Chapter 18

All Aglow

It was 1993, and I was living with another Steven in my life, a man who would soon become my fourth husband, and I was pregnant with my only daughter. My best friend lived next door and she encouraged me to find an outlet, something for myself.

I had a blended family, with my two sons, his two sons, our son, and a daughter on the way! I had chosen to be a stay-at-home mom. I loved being with my children, but sometimes it was all a bit overwhelming, having so many children in the house with no one else to talk to.

I went searching for Women's Aglow, as I remembered my mother introducing me to their organization years before. As it turned out, there was a local chapter in Clear Lake, Texas, and I began attending the monthly meetings. The website describes Aglow as "Up close and personal: that's a good way to describe Aglow Bible studies. A small group meets together regularly to study the Bible and share issues and questions that touch hearts. Bible studies are an especially good place for new Christians to come together with other believers to explore God's Word and put the timeless truths into action in their own personal lives."

It was at the Aglow Bible studies that I became reacquainted with my Lord. The Aglow chapter became my family of sisters who helped me learn and grow in the things of God. I was invited to go to a retreat with them about a year after my daughter Sarah was born, and all I could think was, "There's no way; I have six children at home, and I cannot leave them for the weekend."

Our Aglow president, who had become one of my closest friends, told me to pray about it. When I did, I immediately thought of my sister, Sheila. She lived in Austin and had two small children of her own, and when I told her about the retreat, she did not hesitate to volunteer to come stay with them for the weekend. Aglow paid for everything that weekend. It was the true beginning of a new life with the Lord.

I began going to Bible studies when I could and reading the Word and really exploring this new relationship with God, and to be with a bunch of God-centered women, it really impacted my life. I became close to the women in my chapter, the Nasa chapter, and they became my lifeline to the Lord.

God seemed to be accelerating my learning capacity and through many life lessons, I came to know Him in so many ways. He became my best friend, my deliverer, my provider, and He was already my healer.

Chapter 19

A New Beginning

Here I was, 37 years old, clean, sober, and hopefully wiser, beginning a new life with God at the helm, going on a retreat with my Aglow sisters. I found my calling, my purpose, a good church, and began to be taught by the Holy Spirit to walk with Him. One of the first things God did was to tell me to go ahead and marry the second man I was living with.

We were planning to marry eventually, but didn't have the money, but when I returned home from the retreat, I knew God would provide. We planned to be married two months later and everything came together. I got help from my Aglow sisters, and we had a beautiful wedding under the gazebo of a friend. We rented tuxedos for all the boys and found beautiful dresses for the girls. Sarah was two at the time. She and my niece, Raven, who was nine, were my flower girls. I made the wedding cake, and my friends helped make the food. I found my wedding dress through a family friend and only paid $15.00 for it, and the amazing thing was that it was exactly what I had pictured in my mind! God provided, and we did it all for under $500.00. It was beautiful!

A couple of years later, we had to move out of the house we had been renting and find another, which was not easy with our limited budget and six kids. When I did find a house big enough and cheap enough, they didn't want to rent to us because we were so many. I searched and searched, trying to grab the paper early each day before the good deals were taken.

Finally, a week before we had to move, I found it. The ad said it was a four-bedroom, two-bath for $650.00 a month! That was $75.00 less than we were paying for a three-bedroom! I called and asked if I could see the house. They said they were working on it, but I could come look if I didn't mind the mess. I got there as fast as I could! When I arrived, the landlord and his wife were cleaning. As we talked, I found that the previous renters had been there almost 20 years. I told them we had six children and asked if that would be a problem.

I'll never forget what his wife said that day. She said, "That's not a problem for me, I don't live with them!" Great answer, and the house was huge. It was on a cul-de-sac and had a big front yard and an even bigger fenced backyard. The landlord said he had to replace the tile in the kitchen and bathrooms and that might take a while. When I called my husband with the details, he said he could lay the tile if they would rent it to us immediately. They agreed and we began moving right away. This house was truly an answer to our prayers. God provided bigger, better, and more affordable. We had great neighbors, who became like family through the nine years we lived there.

We moved in on December 1st and paid all the deposits on the utilities, and we were tapped out, but God wasn't! I told all the kids that we probably wouldn't be able to get them much for Christmas because we had to use all our money and our last check to move. The kids were all fine with this, but God had a plan.

Chapter 20

Winning With God

About a week later, my husband asked me to help him pick up a car at an auction. He was working for a wholesaler, and they bought cars at different auctions, fixed them, and resold them. We had to go all the way on the other side of Houston, so it was an hour drive back in a car by myself.

I was spending time with the Lord, and He asked me what I feared most, Him or man. I said, "You, Lord," and that was all He said about that. When we got back to the lot, He told me to give my husband a "word." This was a hard thing for me to do, as my husband wasn't where I was spiritually and had stopped going to church with us. But, in obedience, I stepped out.

God was gracious to me. All I had to tell him was that God loved him very much! Whew!!

So, I got back in our car to go home to the kids; the older teens were watching the little ones. As I headed home, I heard the Lord say to me, "Let's go shopping." I said "Lord, you know I don't have any money or credit cards." He said, "That's okay, you are going to win your purchase." That's all I needed to hear! We headed to Venture, a huge department store. They were having a promotion, where every 50th customer won their entire purchase.

I went shopping with God, and He helped me pick out gifts for the entire family, even a nice Christmas outfit for each of us. We stayed in the store for over an hour while God directed me here and there. At one point, the enemy tried to whisper in my ear, "What if you don't win?" I said aloud, "That's not an option," and continued.

It was Christmas time, so it was really busy, and at one point an employee offered to get me another cart and bring the one I had to the front for me. I was loading up, after all I had six children to buy for. I didn't want to be greedy, so I only got them each one gift, but I didn't realize at the time that I could have got them more, because our Father is an extravagant God!

There I went, pushing my second cart to the front

and asked God which line to get in. He highlighted a cashier that I had been ministering to each time I would come into the store. As I stood in her line, another line opened, and they tried to get me to move over. I told the lady behind me, "You go ahead; I am where I am supposed to be." Halfway through my purchase, they came and told me and the cashier that I was the 50th customer and had won my entire purchase! I screamed out, "Praise God!!" I was having a worship service right there in that line as she continued to ring up both of my baskets. The total came to $1,062.02!!

I can't tell you how much fun it was to shop with the Lord that day! I still have the receipt. I had to bring my car to the door to get help loading everything. I was driving this big old Lincoln Town car, and it was stuffed. I drove over to my husband's office because I didn't want the kids to see everything. When I got there, he was gone, so I asked the other employee if I could leave everything there. We put all the gifts in an empty office, and when I was ready to leave, I made a copy of the certificate they gave me that said I won, with the total on it.

He was blown away when I told him my story, and I knew Steve would be too. As a matter of fact, when he got back, they told him I had 'bought' everything and didn't show him the certificate. Boy, was he mad!! He thought I had found a way to spend money we didn't have. I had a lot of explaining to do that night, but he finally believed that I had won, but not that God had told me to go. He said, "You act like you talk to God, like you talk to me." I said, "I do!"

God is always talking to us, but we are not always listening. The Bible says that God is a friend that sticks closer than a brother, and that's the kind of relationship He wants with us, to be a friend. I was working at a restaurant in Kemah at that time, and when I went to work a couple nights later, one of the other waitresses said she had also won her purchase but had put one item back at the last minute because she didn't have enough money and didn't know she was going to win. That's when I told her my testimony and told her that I knew I was going to win!

What a lesson of God's love, His faithfulness, His blessings in our obedience, and a testimony of hearing His voice!! I became a witness at the restaurant I worked at, in many ways. God had been working on my integrity, and I became a witness by the way I lived. I was no longer the girl who was looking for love and acceptance. I was no longer the one who tried to please everyone else. I was no longer the victim of the lies the enemy had taunted me with; I was a redeemed, cleansed, forgiven child of the One True God, who loves me where I am and who I am.

It is amazing what God will do when you give Him

your life, when you give Him all the pain and broken-
ness of who you were and allow Him to change you
into who you were always meant to be!

Chapter 21

Learning True Integrity in My Walk with Christ

What is integrity? The dictionary says it is an adherence to moral and ethical principles, soundness of moral character, and honesty. Where do we get these principles from? The world's standards are different from the Biblical standards, so if we don't read the Word and learn integrity from it, we follow the world's view, which is totally askew. We need a firm foundation.

For example, the world says it's okay to lie if it suits our purpose. Let's say you are really not feeling like going to work, so you call in sick, but you're not sick. We say that's a "little white lie." Or say someone calls your home phone and you don't want to talk to that person, and you have someone else tell them you are not home, just a "trivial lie." Are these lies, okay? What do our actions say to our kids or anyone else watching us? Is this behavior acceptable because the world says it's, okay?

I hear people say, "Everybody lies sometimes." What does the Bible say about lies? First, it says in Numbers 23:19 and 1 Samuel 15:29 that God is not a man that He should lie. Ouch! So, mankind has the natural characteristic of being a liar? The Bible also calls Satan "the Father of lies" in John 8:44. If we are to be imitators of Jesus, shouldn't we look at His life? Do we think Jesus lied when it suited His purpose? I think not. He said, "When you see me, you see the Father." He was, and still is, our picture of God. I believe that Jesus lived a holy and pure life while on this earth.

The Bible says we are to be in the world, but not of the world. 1 John 2:16 says, "For everything in the world—the lust of the flesh, the lust of the eyes, and the pride of life—comes not from the Father but from the world." That paints a pretty dark picture! I don't know about you, but I would rather look like Jesus than the world!

And that was the whole point of me working at the restaurant for a season. You see, the owner of this particular restaurant actually went to my church and was on the prayer team, meaning he was one of the people whom the congregation went to for prayer. But this man had a problem with alcohol and was not a good example of Godly living. The young people that worked there were in their early twenties and thought it was acceptable to go to a table with a beer in one hand and an alcoholic drink in the other, trying to witness to people about Jesus! He would gossip about others and join in with the crude jokes, trying to be accepted in their groups.

I, on the other hand, had gone through some serious pruning in these areas and when I would walk up to someone who was telling a dirty or off-color joke, they would stop, out of respect. I told them from the get-go that I didn't like that kind of talk, and they didn't put me down for it but gave me honor as I had given God honor. I'm not telling you this to make me look good or anyone else look bad, but as an example of what we are supposed to look like, who we are supposed to model.

This wasn't who I was years ago, at the beginning, but through the years of submission to the Lord, it is who I have become. God is the potter, and we are the clay. When we allow Him to mold us into the vessel He wants, we become a better person and look more like Him! I don't drink, and that was also a big deal to the people I was impacting with my life, though I didn't know how much. The owner would take several of the wait staff to a catering job, and when they would get finished, they would come back to the restaurant, and he would "reward" them by giving them alcohol. They thought it was a totally acceptable trait for a Christian and they thought it was a great bonus. The Word tells us not to be a stumbling block to others, and I have seen firsthand that you don't always know what a person can fall victim to. Some people have addictive tendencies, and we don't always know that. One drink of wine might not affect me, but it might be the catalyst that throws someone else into a world of alcoholism. Or I might be able to take a painkiller for a bad tooth, but my neighbor may be the one that gets hooked on prescription drugs. Only God knows the heart, the mind, or the background of others.

I don't know all the details of the year I spent at the restaurant, how it impacted the others, but I do know that two of the young women and one man all returned to the Lord. I still remember the day one of the ladies called me a couple of years later and thanked me. I was surprised to hear from her, because we had lost touch, but she was grateful for the example of my lifestyle in the restaurant. I am thankful that God chose me to show how He wants us to live. I'm not perfect yet, but I'm not where I used to be. I'm being changed from glory to glory, to look like my Father.

I went to Bible studies at my church, and I was not only learning about God but learning vital Christian disciplines that are necessary to living a Christ-centered life, such as reading the Bible. How can we know what God is like, or even who He is, if we don't read about Him and study about Him? The Bible tells you about God's nature and character, but it is so much more than that. I've heard it said that God's Word is His story, and that is so true! It is the story of creation, how the world was formed from the beginning of time, and it tells of God's creation of man and every living creature. It tells of man's fall from grace and God's redemptive plan to bring us back into relationship with God. That was God's plan from the beginning, to have a people that would be in relationship with Him, to be His family!

When Adam and Eve sinned, they damaged the relationship of the Father with His children. God was not taken by surprise with this; the Bible says in Revelation 22:13 He is "the Alpha and the Omega, the First and the Last, the Beginning and the End." If He knows the beginning from the end, then He knows everything in the middle! He knew Lucifer would betray Him and become the Father of lies. Isaiah 14:12-15 speaks of his fall.

God knew the sneaky devil would tempt Eve, and she and her husband would sin, but God had given them a free will. God allows us to exercise that will, even when our choices are not for our good. God had a plan for redemption, for mankind's redemption from the beginning, even before He created man.

How do we know His will? By spending time reading the Word of God and praying to God. These are just two of the disciplines we have as Christians to follow. We don't just become a Christian by going to church, even though it helps to go to a good Bible-believing church; we have to get to know the Word of God and know the God of the Word.

We need to know what the Bible says about forgiveness, for example: The Old Testament says in Exodus 21:24 "an eye for an eye..." but that is not what Jesus taught in the New Testament, under the New Covenant. In Matthew 18:21-35 Jesus told His disciples a story about a servant that teaches us about forgiveness.

Mathew 18:21-35:

Then Peter came to Jesus and asked, "Lord, how many times shall I forgive my brother or sister who sins against me? Up to seven times?" Jesus answered, "I tell you, not seven times, but seventy times seven." Therefore, the kingdom of heaven is like a king who wanted to settle accounts with his servant. As he began the settlement, a man who owed him ten thousand bags of gold was brought to him. Since he was not able to pay, the master ordered that he and his wife and his children and all that he had be sold to repay the debt. At this the servant fell on his knees before him. "Be patient with me," he begged, "and I will pay back everything." The servant's master took pity on him, canceled the debt, and let him go. But when that servant went out, he found one of his fellow servants who owed him a hundred silver coins. He grabbed him and began to choke him. "Pay back what you owe me!" he demanded. His fellow servant fell to his knees and begged him, "Be patient with me, and I will pay it back." But he refused. Instead, he went off and had the man thrown into prison until he could pay the debt. When the other servants saw what had happened, they were outraged and went and told their master everything that had happened. Then the master called the servant in. "You wicked servant," he said, "I canceled all that debt of yours because you begged me to. Shouldn't you have had mercy on your fellow servants as I had on you?" In anger his master handed him over to the jailers to be tortured, until he paid back all he owed. This is how my heavenly Father will treat each of you unless you forgive your brother or sister from your heart."

God taught me about forgiveness in His time when He knew I was ready to forgive. I had to make a choice to forgive my ex-husband for the abuse he inflicted on me, and that was one of the hardest things I ever did! I would say it over and over, "God, I forgive him," until one day, I truly felt it in my heart, and released him.

I remember where I was when I did it, and it released both of us from the bonds of unforgiveness.

God helped me to truly forgive my mom and get rid of all the anger and bitterness that I had pushed down in my heart for so many years. Mom and I truly became best friends and prayer partners. When I would go to visit her, she couldn't wait to introduce me to her friends. She was proud of the woman I had become in Christ and proud of the way I walked in the calling of the prophet that the Lord had placed on me. She and my dad have gone to be with the Lord, but I know I will see them again when my time on earth is done. In the meantime, I am going to follow God's will for my life and go and do and be all that God desires of me. I am going to shout to the nations, "You are not who the world says you are, but you are who God says you are."

If you are a child of God, a person who has been saved by His grace and given your life to Him, then you are a new creation according to 2 Corinthians 5:7. If you are not saved and have not said the words yet, but would like to be saved, repeat after me, aloud: "Lord, Your Word says that all have sinned and fallen short of the glory of God. I confess with my mouth that I am a sinner and ask You to forgive me of all my sins. I repent and turn from my sin, and I receive Your forgiveness. I believe that Jesus is the Christ, the Son of the One true God, and I believe that He was born of a virgin, was crucified, died, and buried, and on the third day He rose from the grave to give me forgiveness of sin, healing for the body and mind, and the gift of eternal life. I accept Jesus into my heart and ask You to be Lord of my life. I give You all I am and ask You to give me all You have for me, including the baptism of the Holy Spirit, with the evidence of speaking in tongues." Hallelujah!! If you just prayed that prayer for the first time (and really meant it!), you are now a child of God. You have been adopted into His family.

Romans 8:13-16 says, "For if you live according to the sinful nature, you will die; but if by the Spirit you put to death the misdeeds of the body, you will live, because those who are led by the Spirit of God are sons of God. For you did not receive a spirit that makes you a slave again to fear, but the Spirit of sonship. And by Him we cry, 'Abba Father'. The Spirit Himself testifies with our spirit that we are God's children."

As children of God, we don't have to accept what the world, our friends, or even our family says about us. God sees us through the blood of His Son Jesus, and through that blood, we are redeemed (Psalms 107:2), forgiven (Colossians 1:13 & 14), and healed (1 Peter 2:24). We are fearfully and wonderfully made (Psalm 139:14). We are free of the past and free to live life to the fullest!

God has great plans for our lives. Plans that He made from before He even formed us in our mother's womb. The Bible says He knew us, but the enemy, God's enemy, and our enemy, Satan, has come to steal, kill, and destroy our lives. We cannot allow him to do that!! We are worth more than anything in the world to God.

For years, I allowed the enemy to speak lies into my life because I didn't know how to take a stand against him. I didn't have a foundation in the Word.

God says we are His precious possession, more valuable than even the birds of the air. Matthew 6:26 says: "Look at the birds of the air; they do not sow or reap or store away in barns, and yet your heavenly Father feeds them. Are you not more valuable than they?"

You are more valuable than the birds, or rubies, or gold. You are priceless. Jesus paid the ultimate price for you, and for me. Find a good youth group or Bible study (free on Aglow.org website), connect with a God-fearing church, and most importantly, pray and read the Bible. There are resources everywhere!! Don't be afraid to search them out. If you were brave enough to read this book to the end, YOU are brave enough to take hold of everything GOD has for you!

BE BOLD, BE FEARLESS!! BECAUSE YOU ARE HIS!!

Chapter 22

WALK IT OUT

If we are free from the past, how do we live it? We must find out who we are 'in Christ'. The Bible says in Romans 8:14-17 *"For as many as are led by the Spirit of God, these are the sons of God. For you did not receive the spirit of bondage again to fear, but you received the Spirit of adoption by whom we cry out, Abba, Father. The Spirit Himself bears witness with our spirit that we are children of God, and if children of God, then heirs-heirs of God, and joint heirs with Christ, if indeed we suffer with Him, that we also may be glorified together."*

We have got to get that down in our heart, our spirit, and our mind that we are God's children when we become saved. According to Gal. 3:13 "Christ has redeemed us from the curse of the law, having become a curse for us, (for it is written, cursed is everyone who hangs on a tree), that the blessing of Abraham might come upon the Gentiles in Christ Jesus, that we might receive the promise of the Spirit through faith."

Romans 12:2 tells us:
"...and be not conformed to this world: but be transformed by the renewing of your mind that you may prove what is that good and acceptable will of God."

You may be wondering how to do that, and I wondered the same thing. To renew your mind, you not only have to put in new thoughts in your mind, but you also must get rid of old thoughts. We must make a decision to change the way we think. I took that old thought that said I was worthless and replaced it with thoughts and scripture that said the opposite.

When I would start thinking I was worthless I would have to change that thought and replace it with this thought, "I am not worthless, that's a lie. I was created by God, and I am a child of God, a new creation. I am worthy because God says I am worthy. I am loved because God's Word says I am loved."

God wants us to live differently than the world, different from the way we used to live, free from sin, free from lies, free from curses, free from poverty and lack, and free from sickness.

1 Peter 2:24 says:
"...who Himself bore our sins in His own body, that

*we, having died to sins, might live for righteousness --
by whose stripes you were healed."*

If we keep our eyes on Jesus and read the Word and
pray, God will guide us and change us into His image,
day by day, from the inside out. But that doesn't
mean we get a free pass to sin. No, it means we have
been forgiven from past sins, but it is up to us to live
differently, with God's help.

Let me give you an example from my life; I used
to smoke about a pack of cigarettes every day. When
I got saved, God took the desire out of me, and I quit
cold turkey!! I was free for many years, and then I
made the choice to pick them up again and went right
back to the addiction. I smoked cigarettes for another
fifteen years, quitting from time to time until I recom-
mitted my life back to God and stopped forever 12
years ago.

Now I know some will ask if smoking is a sin,
and I say that's a loaded question. The Bible doesn't
specifically say it is, but it does say our bodies are a
temple of the Holy Spirit. 1 Corinthian 3:16 "Do you
not know that you are the temple of God and that the
Spirit of God dwells in you?" So, if we realize that He
is inside us, shouldn't we take care of our bodies and
not abuse them? And I know it is not an easy habit
to break, but the first thing we have to do is submit
it to the Lord and ask for His help, but of course the

best thing is never to start smoking! I started in High School thinking it would make me cool, but when I look back, the ones who smoked were the only ones who thought so!

There will always be something in our life that we can work on, to be a better person, whether it's morally, spiritually, or even physically. The question I would ask you, are you happy and at peace with the person you are at this moment? I always felt that I was never good enough, I never felt loved or loveable because of my childhood. I used to have the attitude, "if they don't like me the way I am, that's their problem." The real down-deep problem was I didn't like me!

So how did I get from there to here? I found my identity in Christ. I found out that God loved me just the way I was but loved me too much to leave me that way. He knew I could be a better person, and love others better, if I was complete in Him.

First: you have to recognize the mindset you are dealing with on a regular basis, mine was feeling unloved. So, I began to look up scriptures that told me God loved ME. I got it that He is love, but my question is, "Does He really love me; Agnes?"

1 John 4:9 says:
"This is how God showed His love among us. He sent

His one and only Son into the world that we might live through Him."

1 John 4:10 says:
"This is love: not that we loved God, but that He loved us and sent His Son as an atoning sacrifice for our sins."

Proverbs 8: 17 says "I love those who love me, and those who seek me find me."

The list goes on and on and studying those love scriptures of how He loves us is the first step.

Second: get rid of the old thoughts! That was what turned the tables on the enemy. I had to take those old thoughts that I was speaking and renounce and reject them and then replace them with good thoughts. For example, saying out loud, "I am not stupid, I have the mind of Christ according to 1 Corinthians 2 which says, *"But we have the mind of Christ." Romans 15:5 says "Now may the God of patience and comfort grant you to be like-minded toward one another, according to Christ Jesus, that you may with one mouth glorify the God and Father of our Lord Jesus Christ."*

Now personalize it: "Now may the God of patience and comfort grant me to be Christ like or Christ minded toward each other, according to Christ Jesus, that I may with one mind and one mouth glorify the God and Father of my Lord Jesus Christ."

Say aloud "I am an intelligent person, and according to Ecclesiastes 1:13 I applied my mind to study and to explore by wisdom all that is done under the heavens."

According to:
2 Timothy 2:15." "I will study to show myself approved."

Psalm 119:15 "I meditate on your precepts and consider your ways."

We can change our lives and set the course of our days when we issue decrees over ourselves. What we say does matter. It can be seen in the lives of the abused in a negative manner and in the lives of successful people in a positive manner.

Proverbs 23:7 tells us, "as a man thinks in his heart so is he."

We've heard it over and over: what you think about and dwell on, you become. If we watch movies with curse words and hang out with people who curse, sooner or later it will come out of our mouths. What we put in always comes out.

I'd rather dwell on the good than the bad. I want to wake up in the mornings in a good mood, looking forward to the new day, not dreading it. I'm a happy, optimistic person, and I like to surround myself with that kind of person. I want to be the person who brings a smile and laughter to others, and that kind of outlook begins with me and the things I say and meditate on, the things I read, watch, and listen to.

Everything in our environment has an effect on us, either for good or evil, and we have a choice in the matter. I choose not to listen to gossip or rumors, even when those around me do, and I try to avoid those places where it's happening. I try not to get pulled into the negative on social media and have blocked others off my pages because of the negativity.

I only listen to Christian music because I don't like the lyrics in most secular music. I do like different styles of music, like rap and hip-hop and even rock and roll, but the words don't keep me uplifted and clean, so I only listen to Christian artists, and there are plenty out there. I'm careful about the type of movies and TV shows I watch. I don't watch R-rated shows and movies, and if I turn something on and they're cursing or doing something I don't agree with morally, I'll turn it off or change the channel.

I don't want to get comfortable or complacent in my walk with the Lord, and when we adopt the ways of the world, that's what happens. Too many times we make excuses like, "Everyone talks like that" or "Everyone is doing it." But I'm telling you, God called us to be different, set apart; the Bible says a peculiar nation.

Titus 3:11-14 says: "For the grace of God that brings salvation has appeared to all men, reaching us that denying ungodliness and worldly lusts, we should live soberly, righteously, and godly in the present age of, looking for the blessed hope and glorious appearing of our great God and Savior Jesus Christ, who gave Himself for us that He might redeem us from every lawless deed and purify us for Himself His own special people, zealous for good works."

We all have a choice to make, even when we don't realize it. We can choose to live like we always have, and get what we always get, or we can choose a better way. Jesus came to give us that choice.

Joshua 24:15 says "But as for me and my house we will serve the Lord."

As I said before, I'm not better than anyone, I'm just different from most. I choose to take the hard road, the road of Christ, the unpopular route.

No, it is not an easy path to follow, and anyone who tells you it is, is a liar. Run the other way! When we decide to live for Christ, the enemy will try everything he can to turn us back to our old ways. He will disrupt our family life, our friends will not understand and turn against us, sometimes even our workplace becomes a battleground, but it is so worth it!!

Walking the Christian walk can be an inward mental battle against our own flesh, and most of the time we are not even aware of it. We live like the world, not making any significant changes in ourselves.

I had a young lady I worked with years ago tell me she knew all about Jesus and what He did, but she didn't want to change her lifestyle. She didn't want to give anything up, especially her parties.

What she didn't realize is what she would gain! Besides giving up poverty for prosperity, sickness for health, feeling unloved for being greatly loved, the biggest thing she was giving up was eternal life. I don't know where she is today, but like so many others, she thinks she has all the time in the world to make that choice. Some even think they can make that choice in the moments of death, but what if you don't have moments or even seconds? We have seen far too many young people in our community die an early death, all the while thinking there would be a tomorrow.

We are not promised tomorrow. We cannot count on even the next moment in time. All we can count on is that we will all see eternity one day, either with the Father, or away from Him. I have authored this book to encourage and hopefully change the lives and outlooks of those who have been beaten down by others, life, or even circumstances.

I am here to tell you there is hope for tomorrow, a hope for a future. God has a plan for our lives, for every single person that has been or ever will be.

Jeremiah 29:11 says: "For I know the thoughts that I think toward you, saith the Lord, thoughts of peace, and not of evil, to give you an expected end."

No matter who you are, or what you have done, or not done, God loves you with a love greater than anything you can imagine and my prayer for you, is that you will reach out to Him, or someone who can lead you to Him. Find a good church and get involved, get a Bible, and read it. If you have never read it before, I would recommend starting in the New Testament with the book of John. I cannot say it enough, YOU ARE LOVED! Stop believing the lies!! God has never given up on you.

Let me tell you some of the things He does not do! He does not lie! He does not put sickness on someone! (He doesn't have it to give!) He doesn't punish us, He redeems us! He does not put poverty on us or want us to live in poverty.

John 10:10 says, "the thief comes only to steal, slaughter, and destroy. I have come that they might have life and have it more abundantly."

John 3:14 - 16 says: "And as Moses lifted up the serpent in the wilderness, even so must the Son of man be lifted up, that whosoever believeth in Him should not perish, but have eternal life, for God so loved the world, that He sent His only Son, that whosoever believeth in Him, should not perish, but have eternal life."

I AM A 'WHOSOEVER,' AND SO ARE YOU!!

Remember, the Bible says that the only way to God is through His Son, Jesus. He is the only one who has died for us, taking our sin and diseases with Him on the cross. He is the only one who was crucified, died and buried, and the only one who rose from the dead, that gives us eternal life.

God loves you. He always will, no matter what. No matter who you are now, or what you may have done, Jesus died to redeem us from ourselves. You matter to God, let Him show you that today.

My prayer for you is that you will let God in and allow Him to love you, just as you are. If He did it for me, He will do it for you. All you must do is receive His love.

May God bless you in your journey!